DATE DUE

1998

PRINTED IN U.S.A.

The United States

Georgia

Paul Joseph
ABDO & Daughters

visit us at
www.abdopub.com

Published by Abdo & Daughters, 4940 Viking Drive, Suite 622, Edina, Minnesota 55435.
Copyright © 1998 by Abdo Consulting Group, Inc., Pentagon Tower, P.O. Box 36036, Minne-apolis, Minnesota 55435 USA. International copyrights reserved in all countries. No part of this book may be reproduced in any form without written permission from the publisher.

Printed in the United States.

Cover and Interior Photo credits: Peter Arnold, Inc., SuperStock

Edited by Lori Kinstad Pupeza
Contributing editor Brooke Henderson
Special thanks to our Checkerboard Kids—Aisha Baker, Matthew Nichols, Morgan Roberts

All statistics taken from the 1990 census; The Rand McNally Discovery Atlas of The United States. Other sources: Compton's Encyclopedia, 1997; *Georgia*, Heinrichs, Children's Press, Chicago, 1989.

Library of Congress Cataloging-in-Publication Data

Joseph, Paul, 1970-
    Georgia / Paul Joseph.
    p. cm. -- (The United States)
    Includes index.
    Summary: Surveys the people, geography, and history of Georgia.
    ISBN 1-56239-854-7
    1. Georgia--Juvenile literature. [1. Georgia.] I. Title. II. Series: United States
    (Series)
    F386.3.J67 1997
    975.8--dc21   97-6873
                                                             CIP
                                                               AC

Contents

Welcome to Georgia

Georgia is the largest state east of the Mississippi River. Georgia's neighbors include Tennessee and North Carolina to the north, Alabama to the west, Florida to the south and deep southwest, and South Carolina and the **Atlantic Ocean** to the east.

For many decades Georgia was known for growing cotton. Now the farmers use the rich Georgia land to grow peanuts, corn, tobacco, pecans, peaches, and much more.

Georgia is named for King George II of England. Georgia is also called the "Empire State of the South." This nickname reflects both Georgia's size and its quick growth in farming and **industry**.

Besides living and working in Georgia, people love to visit the state. People visit the great cities of Atlanta,

Savannah, Augusta, and many more, along with visiting the beautiful **rural** areas of Georgia.

The state of Georgia was on display to the whole world in the summer of 1996, when the Summer Olympics were in Atlanta. The millions of people that came to visit found out why Georgia is such a great state.

Georgia has lakes and mountains.

Fast Facts

GEORGIA
Capital and largest city
Atlanta (394,017 people)
Area
58,060 square miles
(150,375 sq km)
Population
6,508,419 people
Rank: 11th
Statehood
Jan. 2, 1788
(4th state admitted)
Principal rivers
Chattahoochee River,
Flint River,
Savannah River
Highest point
Brasstown Bald; 4,784 feet
(1,458 m)
Motto
Wisdom, justice and moderation
Song
"Georgia on My Mind"
Famous People
James Bowie, Erskine Caldwell,
Jimmy Carter, Joel Chandler
Harris, Martin Luther King, Jr.,
Sidney Lanier, Margaret Mitchell

Georgia is one of the original 13 colonies

13

State Flag

Cherokee Rose

Live Oak

Brown Thrasher

About Georgia

The Peach State

Detail area

Georgia's abbreviation

Borders: west (Alabama, Florida), north (Tennessee, North Carolina), east (South Carolina, Atlantic Ocean), south (Florida)

Nature's Treasures

At one time forests covered all of Georgia. Today, timber still covers 40,000 square miles (103,600 sq km) of the state. Georgia is a leader in forestry and wood **research**.

Because of research, people found new uses for Georgia pine forests. They discovered how to make newsprint from pine.

Georgia has about 48,000 farms. While cotton is still one of the top cash **crops**, many other crops are grown too.

Corn is almost everywhere. The state is the leading **producer** of peanuts and peaches in the U.S. Georgia also grows tobacco, soybeans, oats, hay, watermelon, and cantaloupes, to name a few.

The weather is another treasure of Georgia. Because of the wonderful weather, farming is excellent in the state. The weather also brings in many **tourists** who enjoy the mild winter, the warm spring and fall, and the hot summer.

Peaches growing in Georgia's warm sun.

Beginnings

Long before Europeans came to Georgia, the peace-loving Cherokee and Creek **Native Americans** lived there.

Around 1540, Hernando de Soto of Spain passed through the area and **claimed** the area for Spain. In 1732, King George II and England claimed the land.

The English founded a colony where many poor Germans and Austrians lived. It was also a defense area used against the Spanish who were living in Florida.

After many wars in which Georgia was the major battlefield, it became part of the United States. On January 2, 1788, Georgia became the fourth state in the Union.

In the 1860s, Georgia was a big part of the **Civil War**. A large part of the state was destroyed and burned. Georgia rebuilt slowly after the war.

Today, Georgia is part of the "New South." The capital of the state, Atlanta, is the birthplace of Martin Luther King, Jr. It is also thought to be the heart of the **Civil Rights Movement**.

Spanish troops and Native Americans near Macon, Georgia.

B.C. to 1500s

The Land and People

Before 1500, forests covered all of Georgia. Cherokee and Creek **Native Americans** lived in Georgia.

1540: Hernando de Soto marches through parts of Georgia. He **claims** it for Spain.

Georgia

B.C. to 1500s

1700s to 1930

Statehood and Beyond

1788: On January 2, Georgia becomes the fourth state.

1793: Eli Whitney invents the cotton gin near Savannah.

1929: Civil Rights leader Martin Luther King, Jr., is born in Atlanta.

Georgia

1700s to 1930

1970s to Present

Present-Day Georgia

 1976: Jimmy Carter, born in 1924 in Plains, is elected 39th president of the United States.

 1980: The world's largest airport terminal opens in Atlanta.

 1995: The Atlanta Braves win the World Series.

 1996: Atlanta hosts the Summer Olympics.

Georgia

1970s to Present

Georgia's People

There are about 6.5 million people that live in Georgia. Only 10 other states are larger than Georgia. During the 1980s, Georgia was one of the fastest growing states.

Before Georgia became part of the United States, mostly Cherokee and Creek **Native Americans** lived there. Today, there is a large mixture of races that live in the state.

Many famous people have lived in Georgia. Atlanta is the birth place of the civil rights leader, Martin Luther King, Jr. He was **assassinated** in 1968. His gravesite and memorial are located in Atlanta.

Jimmy Carter, the 39th president of the United States, was born in the tiny **rural** town of Plains. Before becoming president he was a peanut farmer and the governor of Georgia.

*Civil rights leader
Dr. Martin
Luther King, Jr.*

*39th United States
President
Jimmy Carter*

Splendid Cities

Atlanta is the capital of Georgia and its largest city. Many people are making this beautiful city their home. In 1986, Gwinnett County, in which part of Atlanta resides, was the fastest-growing county in the nation. The city hosted the 1994 **Super Bowl** and the 1996 Summer Olympic Games.

With the city being the home of the late Martin Luther King, Jr., Atlanta is thought to be the heart of the **Civil Rights Movement**. It is also home to many growing businesses. Coca Cola is the most famous business in the city.

The second largest city in Georgia is Columbus. It is an **industrial** city located on the Chattahooche River. Savannah is a beautiful historic city located on the **Atlantic Ocean**.

20

Macon is in the middle of the state and has many cotton, knitting, and lumber mills. The splendid city of Augusta is on the Savannah River. The resort city is world famous because of the Masters professional golf tournament.

Atlanta, Georgia

Georgia's Land

Georgia's area is 58,060 square miles (150,375 sq km), including 1,011 square miles (2,618 sq km) of water surface. Georgia has five very different regions of land.

The Coastal Plains occupy about half of Georgia's land. It has hills, rivers, streams, marshes, and swamps. Also, sandy areas known as pine barrens are where many longleaf pines grow.

The Piedmont **Plateau** covers about 30 percent of Georgia. This area has most of the large cities. Also many farms are in this region. Besides cities and farms, there are rivers, mountains, forests, and valleys.

The Blue Ridge is an area in Georgia with mountains and valleys. The Blue Ridge averages 2,000 to 3,000 feet (610 m to 914 m) above sea level. Brasstown Bald Mountain, the highest point in the state, has an elevation of 4,784 feet (1,458 m).

The Valley and Ridge region is a small area of mountains. The area is covered with many kinds of rocks. Some types of rocks are very weak, so water running over them wears down these rocks. Some types of rocks are strong. Water can't **erode** these as easily.

The Cumberland **Plateau** has two broad, flat-topped ranges. Lookout Mountain and Sand Mountain, which are divided by a narrow valley.

Okefenokee Swamp

Georgia at Play

Georgia's sunshine, warmth, mountains, valleys, and waters bring thousands of people into this beautiful state.

With this wonderful land, people can have a lot of fun. People can fish, boat, camp, and hike. There are national forests with very old trees.

There are islands and prairies with streams running through them. People can take boat rides through these water trails. In parks, people can also see swamps and wildlife from wooden walkways.

Georgia has many historic sites. American **Civil War** battlefields are preserved at Kennesaw Mountain National Battlefield Park.

Georgia is home to beautiful golf courses, including the world-famous Augusta National. If you like to watch sports, Georgia has a lot of action. The professional teams that play there are the Hawks in basketball, the Falcons in football, and the Braves in baseball.

Fishing is a favorite pastime in Georgia.

Georgia at Work

The people of Georgia must work to make money. Many of the jobs are in **tourism**, **military**, **government**, and service. Service is cooking and serving food, working in banks or stores, and doing many other things for the people of Georgia.

A lot of Georgians farm, mine, or fish. With **48,000** farms, Georgia grows a lot of the food we eat. Georgia farmers grow more peanuts and peaches than any other state.

In mining, Georgia is the leader in **producing** china clay. Georgians also mine cement, sand and gravel, iron ore, and coal. Fishermen catch and sell shrimp, blue crab, and other sea life.

In Atlanta, many people work for Coca Cola. The biggest news station in the world is in Atlanta. Cable News Network (CNN) employs thousands.

Today, Georgia is growing because of its beauty, jobs, and climate. The Empire State of the South is a great place to visit, live, work, and play.

Iron mining is big business in Georgia.

Fun Facts

•In 1786, Augusta was named the first capital of Georgia. It was moved to Louisville in 1796, then Milledgeville in 1807. In 1868, Atlanta became the fourth and final capital.

•The highest point in Georgia is Brasstown Bald. It is 4,784 feet (1,458 m) tall.

•Georgia is the 21st largest state in land size. It is 58,060 square miles (150,375 sq km).

•Georgia received two professional sports teams in 1966. The Braves baseball team and the Falcons football team played their first seasons in Atlanta.

The State Capitol building in Atlanta, Georgia.

Glossary

Assassinated: to murder, especially a very important person, by sudden attack.

Atlantic Ocean: one of a few large seas that surround continents. This one borders the entire east coast of the U.S., including part of Georgia.

Civil Rights Movement: people fighting for equal rights.

Civil War: a war between groups within the same country. In the United States it was war between the North and the South.

Claim: to take for yourself or call your own.

Crops: what farmers grow on their farm to eat and sell.

Erode: to wear away.

Government: working for the country, state, city, or county.

Industry: any kind of business.

Military: working within the armed forces, such as the army or navy.

Native Americans: the first people who were born in and occupied North America.

Plateau: an area of flat land that is raised above the surrounding area.

Produce: to make something.

Research: to hunt for facts or truth.

Rural: no cities around, out in the country.

Super Bowl: the championship of the National Football League.

Tourism: an industry that serves people who are traveling for fun, and visiting places of interest.

Tourists: people who travel for fun.

Internet Sites

Georgia Index
http://valuecom.com/georgia
This site has information on Georgia's history, geography, state flag, and the same information you would find in an encyclopedia.

Georgia On My Mind
http://www.iarc.com/georgia/code/welcome.html
The Georgia Information center. This site has lots of information and links on things Georgian.

Georgia Info
http://www.cviog.uga.edu/Projects/gainfo
A World Wide Web Resource for Georgia Citizens and Public Officials. Contains general information, Georgia maps, Voter Information as well as sites on Georgia Government, counties, and cities.

These sites are subject to change. Go to your favorite search engine and type in Georgia for more sites.

PASS IT ON

Tell Others Something Special About Your State

To educate readers around the country, pass on interesting tips, places to see, history, and little unknown facts about the state you live in. We want to hear from you!

To get posted on ABDO & Daughters website E-mail us at "mystate@abdopub.com"

Index